DIANE LINKLETTER

a
princess
wrongly
accused

DIANE LINKLETTER

a princess wrongly accused

TOM BLEECKER

Gilderoy Publications
Menifee, California

Copyright © by Tom Bleecker

All rights reserved. No part of this book may be reproduced by any mechanical, photographic, or electronic process, or in the form of a phonographic recording; nor may it be stored in a retrieval system, transmitted, or otherwise be copied for public or private use—other than for "fair use" as brief quotations embodied in articles and reviews—without prior written permission of the publisher.

This book is designed to provide information on Diane Linkletter only and does not contain all information available on the subject. While every effort has been made to make this book as accurate as possible, there may be content errors. Therefore, this book should serve only as a general guide and not as the ultimate source of subject information. The author and publisher shall have no liability or responsibility to any person or entity regarding any loss or damage incurred, or alleged to have incurred, directly or indirectly, by the information contained in this book. You hereby agree to be bound by this disclaimer or you may return this book for a full refund.

Library of Congress Cataloging-in-Publication Data
Bleecker, Tom 1946-
Diane Linkletter: a Princess Wrongly Accused, Tom Bleecker
p.cm.
ISBN 9781534822023 (trade paper)
Bleecker, Tom 1946- 2. Hollywood celebrity suicide—Art Linkletter—Ed Durston—LSD acid—biography. I. Bleecker, Tom. II. Title.

Designed by Kurt Wahlner, www.wahlner.com

First printing, July 2016

"The great enemy
of the truth is
very often not the lie,
deliberate, contrived
and dishonest,
but the myth,
persistent, persuasive
and unrealistic."

—John F. Kennedy

CONTENTS

introduction | 1

ONE
high school sweethearts | 7

TWO
engagement and a rising star | 17

THREE
shoreham towers | 27

FOUR
chapter 4, 1969 | 37

FIVE
the investigation | 41

SIX
interrogation of grant conroy | 49

SEVEN
october 4, 1969 revisited, part 1 | 61

EIGHT
october 4, 1969 revisited, part 2 | 69

about the author | 79

introduction

It seems like I've been working on this book since the morning of October 4, 1969 when I first learned of Diane's death. More than four decades later, what initially began as my making notes in my head eventually led to my acquiring Diane's autopsy report, police records, and reaching out to the half dozen key people who were around her during the final years of her life.

Since the morning of her death, 30 years had passed before I developed a foundation as an investigative journalist when I wrote *Unsettled Matters: the Life and Death of Bruce Lee*. Coincidentally, I first met Diane in the mid-1960s, around the same time that I became acquainted with Bruce Lee at the 1964 Long Beach Karate Internationals where he gave his legendary kung-fu demonstration that lit the fuse of him skyrocketing to worldwide stardom eight years later.

I was as troubled by Bruce Lee allegedly dying from a single pill that was comparable to aspirin as I was to Diane falling six floors to her death from her kitchen window because she was having a bad trip on LDS.

So, after cutting my teeth on Lee's death, which consumed me for two years and called for me to travel to Hong Kong and other key cities throughout the United States, I finally decided to finish my investigation into Diane's death.

Diane and I first met when we were teenagers attending neighboring high schools in Los Angeles. Within six months, our friendship grew and we became boyfriend and girlfriend—and then within a short time we became engaged to be married.

During the years I was around Diane, I loved and cared for her and was close to her family. Over time, as often occurs in the lives of couples, our career paths went in separate directions, which resulted in our calling off our engagement. Thankfully, we were able to return to being close friends and over the years kept in close touch and occasionally saw each other.

I wish things would have remained that way and that we could have grown old together, enjoying each other's company and often sharing fond memories. But instead, I've lived with the horrible memory of Diane falling to her death from the sixth floor of her apartment. When I first learned of what had happened, I didn't believe the story that the media was reporting. Not then, and not now.

The two aspects of Diane's death that have troubled me for all these years are that (1) she had for years had a serious drug problem (including an addiction to heroin) dating back to when she was 13 years old, and (2) she was deeply despondent, even emotionally distraught, on the morning of her death. Unfortunately, these false beliefs inevitably found their way onto the Internet where they have become part of not only Diane's legacy, but also the legacy of her father Art Linkletter.

Diane Linkletter was never a druggie. When I first met her, she was living with her parents and was in robust health, as emotionally stable as any teenager I knew, consistently maintained a positive outlook on life, and enjoyed a loving relationship with her parents and siblings. Generally speaking, both her home life and her bright future were the envy of many of her peers.

By October 4, 1969, as these pages will establish, Diane was living her dream of becoming a successful actress. This was helped along by her famous father, Art Linkletter, who was a prominent figure throughout the entertainment business. Along with Diane's mother, Lois, Art was enormously proud of Diane and highly supportive of her chosen path in life. On the day she died, this precious young girl had everything to live for. There is absolutely no way that she would have taken her own life.

Moreover, Diane Linkletter did not take LSD on the morning of her death, as was substantiated by the laboratory findings of her autopsy. This came as no surprise to me because in all the time I knew Diane and was around her, I never once—not once—thought that she might have a drug problem.

I've been in and around the Hollywood film and television community for my entire adult life. Even as a child, I was often in the company of people who worked in the Hollywood entertainment business; in fact, I set foot on my first television sound stage at the age of 12 or 13 at Lucille Ball and Desi Arnez's Desilu Studios.

Anyone who has been around the Hollywood film and television industry for as long as I have (55 years), has seen plenty of drug use, as well as the lives it destroys.

Had Diane been a serious drug user, everyone around her, especially her father, would have spotted this because drug abuse is easily recognizable in the user's physical appearance, their emotional state, and their highly-volatile, ever-changing demeanor.

And while many drug addicts believe they are hiding their destructive lifestyle from everyone, the reality is that the signposts and earmarks of a person addicted to drugs hang above their heads like a flashing neon sign. Diane had none of these indicators, and if she had, I have no doubt that her father would have done everything in his power to remedy the problem.

In my view, Diane's death was the result of her being altogether too trusting of people. During the last two years of her life, she made the acquaintance of a group of individuals that she should have watched more closely. Instead, because of her friendly, often accommodating nature, she ignored many warning signs until one day in the wee hours of the morning, she found herself in life-threatening situation that she was unable to control.

Surely, there will be those who will question my motive for writing this small book. The truth is my reason is simply that I felt that someone needed to address the continued damage to Diane and her father's legacies. And if not me, then who?

I felt the same way about Bruce Lee when I wrote *Unsettled Matters*. When Bruce's widow Linda first asked me to write her husband's biography, she said (I paraphrase), "You're the only one who can write this book, Tom. Not only were you Bruce's friend, but you're also a martial artist, someone who has worked in Hollywood for years, and you're a professional writer." And she was right. No one else around Bruce Lee had my shared background with Bruce, as well as my credentials as a writer.

There came a time when I felt the same about Diane. Who else knew her from her early childhood until the day she died, has worked in the Hollywood film and television industry, has the experience as an investigative journalist, and has worked as a professional writer for many decades?

In my view, someone needed to make an effort to correct the wrong that has been done to Diane's legacy. And if not me, then who? My only hope is that I've done a good job because Diane deserves as much.

ONE

high school sweethearts

For nearly 25 years, whenever I'd mention to people that I grew up in the West Los Angeles area of Brentwood and attended Paul Revere Junior High School, they instantly assumed that I was born with a silver spoon in my mouth. I credit this false assumption to O.J. Simpson because of his Brentwood mansion on Rockingham Avenue and the fact that his daughter attended neighboring Paul Revere Junior High School.

Although I did live in Brentwood, along with many of my childhood friends, my parents rented apartments that were located in a one square mile area just north of Wilshire Blvd. between Bundy Drive and Barrington Avenue. Even though I lived in low-cost rented apartments, I was able to attend the best public schools with the kids who came from the wealthy areas of Brentwood and neighboring Trousdale Estates, Bel Air, Pacific Palisades, and the fringes of Beverly Hills.

During my enrollments at Brentwood Elementary School, Paul Revere Junior High School, and University ("Uni") High School, many of my friends were the children of some of the biggest Hollywood celebrities, including Groucho Marks, Frank Sinatra, Gene Berry, Anthony Quinn, Robert Mitchum, Don DeFore, Gregory Peck, and Judy Garland, as well as a dozen A-list directors and producers.

My mother was the main reason our family was uprooted from New Jersey when I was five years old and transplanted in Brentwood. Back in New Jersey, she had entered a string of beauty contests that eventually landed her a chance at competing in the Mrs. America competition after she did well in the Mrs. New Jersey pageant in 1949 and 1950.

After arriving on the fringes of Hollywood in the early 1950s, my mother eventually made several key connections in the entertainment business. As a result, at the age of 13, I made my first television appearance on the popular TV show *The Real McCoys* (starring Walter Brennan) as an extra in a country-style corn eating contest. To my surprise, this black and white show is actually shown today on YouTube.

Although I was enjoying a good time with my friends, my home life was highly dysfunctional. My parents divorced a short while after moving to California and, as a result, I rarely saw my father who, until the late 1950s, was a career military officer.

After living with my mother until I turned 16, our relationship became so strained that my father rented a small 2-bedroom house in Brentwood and I moved in with him. At the time, he was working as a salesman in downtown Los Angeles, and because of the long drive from his office to Brentwood, I rarely saw my dad. Not surprisingly, because of my difficult home life, my grades, as well as my attendance, at University High School began to suffer.

There was one saving grace in my life, however. During the summer of 1962, shortly after I turned 16, I enrolled in Ed Parker's Kenpo Karate School that was located on La Cienega Blvd., which was 10 miles from my home. I did well, and the following year was awarded my brown belt and eventually continued my study at Ed Parker's West Los Angeles school that was closer to Brentwood.

Back in the early 1960s, the exotic art of karate was practically unknown, which is why it attracted an eclectic group of people. The student roster of the advanced class read like *The Wild Bunch* and included a couple of ex-felons, several Hell's Angels, a recent Mr. Universe, and a college football hero, among others. On the tournament circuit, Ed Parker had a group who became known as "The Wrecking Crew." And they fought anyone and everyone. Their most formidable foe was a nearby Tang Soo Do school, whose head instructor was a young man named Chuck Norris. Ed Parker's most notorious black belt hung out in Memphis. His name was Elvis Presley, and he didn't own a guitar upon which our school emblem wasn't prominently displayed. It was a select group of Ed Parker's black belts who later became known as the infamous Memphis Mafia. Men whose sole purpose was to protect "The King."

In August of 1964, after being awarded the highest degree

of brown belt, I competed in the now-legendary Long Beach Karate Internationals where a young Bruce Lee, then a virtual unknown to the rapidly growing karate community, dazzled the packed Long Beach Municipal Auditorium with his extraordinary skills.

The following spring, I was struggling through my senior year at Uni High when the school's football coach caught me smoking in the boy's gym. Fifteen minutes later, I was seated across the desk from Dr. Steinberg, who was the school's boy's vice principal.

The usually cheerful Dr. Steinberg was bald and drew a remarkable resemblance to actor Howie Mandel. This was by no means the first time I sat across the desk from Dr. Steinberg, which is why I didn't offer an excuse, but merely asked how many days I was being suspended. Because the typical suspension was three days, I was certain that I'd be suspended for five.

Steinberg waved my thick file that he had retrieved from his file cabinet, and then slid it in front of me. "I'm not suspending, Tom. You and I have finally come to the end of the road. This time you're being expelled."

What? Although I'd heard the word "expelled," I'd never heard of anyone *being* expelled, and my mother and father had definitely never heard of such a thing. Expulsion from a good school in a neighborhood like Brentwood wasn't supposed to happen to a likeable kid like me, who was voted by his classmates to most resemble blonde teen idol Troy Donahue.

Six months before being shown the door at Uni High, I'd met a wonderful 16-year-old girl named Diane, whose father was Art Linkletter. For those readers who aren't familiar with Art

Linkletter, he was born Arthur Gordon Kelly on July 17, 1912 in Moose Jaw, Saskatchewan, Canada.

Abandoned at birth, he was soon adopted by an evangelical couple who relocated to the United States while Art was a child. Linkletter attended high school in San Diego, where he was a star athlete and graduated at the age of 15. After drifting around the country for many years working as a busboy, meatpacker, and sailor, when he turned 23, he married a wonderful woman named Lois Foerster.

Though educated to be a teacher, Art acquired a better paying job as a radio announcer. In 1955, he cohosted the opening of Disneyland with actor and future US president Ronald Reagan. Linkletter was at the helm of *The Tonight Show* prior to Johnny Carson. He was the host of *House Party*, which ran on CBS radio and television for 25 years, and *People Are Funny* on NBC radio and TV for 19 years. During the 1960s and up until the day he died, Art Linkletter was a household word throughout most of America. In addition, having amassed an estimated net worth of $100-million during his heyday, Art Linkletter was one of the wealthiest celebrities in Hollywood.

Art and Lois had five children together, all raised in the family's luxurious 12,000 sq. ft. 9-bedroom, 9-bath family home on South Mapleton Drive in the exclusive West Los Angeles area known as Holmby Hills (location of the famed Playboy mansion). Around the time I met Diane, she was the only child still living with her parents. All of her four siblings (in order of age)—Jack, Dawn, Robert, and Sharon—had reached adulthood and moved out.

Now that the family was considerably downsized, Art sold the family house on Mapleton Avenue to American composer, conductor and arranger Henri Mancini, who is best remembered for his film and television scores. Just prior to my meeting Diane, Art and his wife moved with Diane into a 3-bedroom, 19th floor penthouse apartment in the exquisite, full service newly-constructed Wilshire Comstock Towers.

Given that I'd just been thrown out of high school, spending time with Diane and her family gave me a sense of much-needed renewed dignity. I'd pull up to the main entrance of the Wilshire Comstock in my father's ten-year-old column-shift 1954 Chevy Bel Air, and then be cleared through to the Linkletter's luxurious penthouse. At the end of the evening, I'd take the elevator down to the marble-floored lobby and stand beneath a row of gleaming crystal chandeliers while my father's car was brought up from the building's underground parking by a white-gloved valet. Moments later, he would hold the driver's door open for me and, with a smile, bid me a good evening.

Diane and I often hung out together in the living room of her parents' penthouse, mostly sitting on the sofa or standing out on the balcony looking out over the city. I can still recall one evening throwing water balloons at the passing city busses below (no doubt Diane's parents weren't home), as well as the night Diane offered to bake a potato for me before we went out. I remember telling her that we didn't have 45 minutes to wait for a baked potato and was surprised, if not baffled, when she demonstrated how their built-in microwave (in 1965, totally new to me) could cook a baked potato in just a few minutes!

When Diane's parents were home, they usually stayed to themselves. Whenever I did see them, they greeted me with a friendly smile and asked how things were going in my life. I don't recall Diane having a curfew, although I always brought her home at a reasonable hour.

During all the time I spent with her, she was always in a great mood, had an extremely positive outlook on life, and was the picture of health. Everyone liked her and enjoyed being around her. Most importantly, I never once saw her use drugs or even take a drink of alcohol. In fact, I don't ever recall the subject coming up.

From all appearances, Diane's parents loved her and were proud of her. In every sense of the word, Diane was a princess.

Diane and I spent time with her parents. In 1963, the building of the Valley Music Theater in Woodland Hills was financed by Art Linkletter, Bob Hope, and Cy Warner, who was an innovative Hollywood club and theater owner during the 1940s, '50s, and '60s.

The 2865-seat facility opened July 6, 1964 with *The Sound of Music*. The first year saw the theater mount 18 musicals, three comedies, a drama, as well as concerts with a combined audience of over 600,000.

To help promote shows, Art and his wife regularly attended performances at the Valley Music Theater, and Diane and I often went with them. Among the best live Broadway musicals that I recall seeing, my favorites were *Seven Brides for Seven Brothers* and *Oklahoma*. Both starred the highly talented singer John Raitt, father of singer Bonnie Raitt.

Around the time I was seeing Diane, she was enrolled in the

elite and very pricy Chadwick School, which was a K-12 co-educational school located on a 45-acre hilltop on the scenic Palos Verdes Peninsula. The school aimed to bring out the best in its students through one-on-one mentoring, unparalleled global opportunities, and an award-winning visual and performing arts program. As was the case with all of Art and Lois Linkletter's children, Diane was afforded the very best of everything.

This was summertime, and Diane and I relished in it. Whenever possible, we spent much of our days at the beaches in Santa Monica and Malibu and many evenings in Westwood Village, particularly at the Village and Bruin theaters. Back then, drive-in movies, as well as drive-in eating places (Truman's and Dolores' were the favorites of our crowd) were popular. During this time, even though I was no longer in high school, I continued living with my father.

Aside from the time I spent with Diane, many of my afternoons and early evening were spent working as a karate instructor at Ed Parker's WLA school. One day, Ed Parker asked if I'd be willing to manage a Kenpo school that he had just opened with his top student Chuck Sullivan that was located in the Crenshaw District. As part of my job, I'd be allowed to live at the school, which many martial artists referred to back then as a "dojo janitor." I wouldn't be the first—or the last—to become a resident manager of a karate school in the mid-1960s when karate was beginning to flourish.

By the end of the week, I informed my father that I'd be heading out to make my mark on the world. Although he didn't have much confidence that I'd make much of a mark without a high school education, he wished me well and said he'd hope for the best. I packed my worldly belongings into a half dozen cardboard boxes and threw them into the back of a lackluster 1950 Cadillac convertible that was on its last legs and moved into the back of the newly-opened Kenpo Karate school on Crenshaw Blvd.

Within two weeks, my routine was well-established. I'd awaken in the morning, shower at a student's house nearby, have breakfast at the local Tiny Naylor's restaurant, then return to the school to answer the phone and teach private lessons. Then in the evening, I'd help Chuck Sullivan teach classes that ranged from beginner to advanced. It wasn't much of a start, but it was a start nonetheless. Thankfully, I had Diane's full support. She believed in me, and we believed in each other.

A short while later, I received my black belt from Ed Parker, which I considered a huge milestone in my life. While I didn't have a high school diploma, I had a black belt diploma that took many years of hard work to obtain. At that time, I was the first student to receive a black belt in the WLA school's legacy and one of the few teenage black belts in the country. Life was good. I was on my own. I had plans, and Diane was a part of them.

TWO

engagement and a rising star

While I was working and living in the back of the Crenshaw school, Diane and I continued to date. After six months, our friendship had blossomed and we officially became boyfriend and girlfriend. Now and then, I'd take a weeknight off from the karate school and drive 10 miles to the Wilshire Comstock to see her. And, of course, we spent weekends together and would often attend parties that were usually held at Chuck Sullivan's home.

Convinced that Diane and I were in love and had a future together, I purchased an engagement ring at Zales Jewelers

(Chuck cosigned because I had no established credit) and proposed to Diane and she accepted. She was 16, and I was 18. We announced our engagement at one of Chuck's parties. To supplement my salary for managing the karate school, I went to work selling insurance for an insurance agency that was located next door to the school.

A week after we became engaged, Diane and I were again going to the Valley Music Theater with her parents. Up until this point, Diane hid her ring from her parents, but this night decided to wear it.

Prior to going to the theater, Diane's father arranged for us to have dinner at the Sportsman's Lodge in Sherman Oaks. As we walked into the Sportsman's Lodge, Diane slipped on her ring. After we were seated in the dining room (by now, my heart rate had doubled), it took a nanosecond for Art and Lois to notice Diane's diamond engagement ring. To my surprise—and temporary relief—neither one of them commented, although Diane and I suspected there may have been some knee nudging under the table.

After leaving the Valley Music Theater, we returned to the Wilshire Comstock. Diane and I went to the living room, and within a few minutes, her mother appeared, smiled, and graciously told me that her husband would like to talk with me.

That evening was the first time I'd been in Art Linkletter's office, which that was located at the far end of the long hall and filled with memorabilia from his many decades of success in both Hollywood and the business world.

Lining the walls were photos taken with US presidents and

major Hollywood stars. Dozens of trophies and plaques were in evidence everywhere. A floor to ceiling bookshelf filled with books was evidence that he was well educated.

I silently thanked my heavenly stars when Diane's father greeted me with a warm smile and asked me to sit across from his desk. After I acknowledged that the ring Diane was wearing was an engagement ring given to her by me, he asked in a general way what my intentions were.

Looking back, I realize that I should have gone about this the proper way and asked him for his daughter's hand in marriage. Why I didn't, I have no idea. Most likely I felt there was a good chance he would say no. But now that I had passed that failsafe point, I told him that I had plans of opening up a chain of karate schools that I felt would be successful, and that eventually I wanted to attend college. Far more important, I told him that I loved his daughter and would do all in my power to make her happy.

With the ball now in his court, while Diane's father didn't formally give Diane and I his blessing, nor did he voice his disapproval. Instead, he simply asked that Diane and I didn't do anything rash, and above all else, in a roundabout way, he made it clear that he'd been raised as a preacher's son who embraced high moral and ethical values. There was no doubt in my mind as to what he was alluding to—hell or high water, I had better not get his daughter pregnant.

After leaving his office, I returned to the living room and told Diane what had transpired—and that the bottom line was that although our engagement was on some sort of trial basis, from what I could tell, she could continue to wear her ring.

We were both overjoyed. Later, she told me that she felt that her father liked me because I was walking a similar path as her father had walked—starting out with nothing more than a tremendous faith in myself and a plan, and that I wasn't afraid of hard work.

There may well have been some truth to this. Looking back over Art's life, two things he once said have stuck in my mind. Having suffered through the Great Depression, Art once recalled, "During the depths of the Depression, you didn't ask what the job was, what the pay was, and you didn't ask about stock options, or—you said yes." The second comment was, "I grew up poor. I never had any money. I was a hobo, you know, I rode the freights."

Diane also mentioned that her mother had told her a while back that she was impressed with my good manners and that I treated her and Diane with respect.

After moving out of the house I shared with my father, I hadn't heard from him for six months when one day I received a letter from him, telling me that he had gotten married. Although we had parted on slightly strained terms, he invited me to come to his home in Glendora to meet his new wife and her three small children.

When we met a week later, I learned that my father's new wife worked as a public school psychologist and was concerned that I hadn't finished high school. It had been some time that I'd been in a real home with a shower, kitchen, and television, so when my dad and his wife offered to have me stay with them and enroll in a private school in West Hollywood called the Colin

McEwen School that would result in my obtaining a high school diploma, I accepted their generous offer.

Throughout the entire time that I was dating Diane and even into our engagement, I never once knew that she was having a difficult time in school. Perhaps she never mentioned this because she realized that I'd been expelled from high school and she simply didn't want to bring up the subject. For whatever reason, I assumed that she had done well at Chadwick and would continue to do so.

Such was not the case, however, and when the fall semester came around, Diane sadly told me that her parents had enrolled her in The Desert Sun School in Idyllwild. For the past 60 years, this college preparatory boarding school had a high success rate of turning unmotivated teenagers into college-bound graduates. Nestled beneath a canopy of pines and oaks, the school had cultivated the children of many of the biggest stars in Hollywood, as well as offspring of many American corporate captains and foreign magnates.

Because I didn't have a reliable car, the two-hour drive to see Diane at The Desert Sun School was difficult on both me and Diane. Back in the mid-1960s, the Internet, text messaging, cellphones, and Skype, which would have made communicating with each other far easier, didn't exist. Unfortunately, because of the strict rules at Desert Sun, something as simple as a standard phone call had to go through channels and be scheduled, because none of the students had their own phone. As a result, the only means by which Diane and I could communicate were handwritten letters sent by snail mail and an all too infrequent phone call or personal visit.

After two sessions at Colin McEwen School, I graduated high school and was able to enroll at Santa Monica City College (SMCC). In addition, I moved out of my father's home in Glendora and into a single apartment at the upscale Barrington Plaza in West Los Angeles.

Although normally there was no way that my father would have foot the pricey rental at this exclusive high-rise, he was able to pay rent with a deeply-discounted "script" that was circulating among business people at that time and used like Monopoly money. In essence, paying with inflated script meant that legally the users didn't have to pay income taxes on that money. In essence, our single apartment that should have cost $1,000 per month actually cost $600 per month.

In the summer of 1967, I moved into a tenth floor single apartment with a roommate from Uni High. While the apartment was small, it came with a sweeping view of the city, an Olympic-sized pool, 24-hour doorman, and three high-rise buildings filled many "cool, happening people."

In addition to my teaching job at the WLA karate school, I took a job as a lifeguard at the prestigious Standard Club in Cheviot Hills, which resulted in my being surrounded by people who were as interesting as my neighbors back at the Barrington Plaza.

Over the past year, I had cultivated a friendship with kung-fu practitioner Bruce Lee, who had, since his appearance at the 1964 Long Beach Internationals, made a huge impression on the martial arts community and was on the verge of breaking into Hollywood's TV industry.

Because I was now personal friends with one of the co-owners of the Barrington Plaza, Don Karnes, I arranged for Bruce and his wife Linda (and their two-year-old son Brandon) to lease a two-bedroom apartment at the Plaza. This also allowed me to work out privately with Bruce Lee, which we often did along with Karnes in whatever vacant apartment was available.

Around this same time, Diane was also undergoing a major change in her life. Her time at Desert Sun had been well spent and resulted in her developing a strong desire to pursue a career in Hollywood. From what she told me, her father was extremely pleased for her and promised to help her in any way he could.

On many levels, the paths Diane and I once traveled together had over the past year somehow split into two separate roads. Although the old adage "absence makes the heart grow fonder" works for many, this was not the case for us, and so we decided to call off our engagement and returned to being friends.

Over the next several months, I continued my studies at SMCC, and for the first time in my life was getting excellent grades. I'd finally reached a point in my education, or lack thereof, that I realized that wearing the hat of the class clown and screw-up that I'd worn in high school had gotten me nowhere in life. My real awakening, however, was when I learned early on that my teachers didn't take attendance. All that really mattered were my grades. Either I earned good grades or I was out, which, thankfully, I took as both an insult and a challenge.

Around that same time, Diane had graduated from The Desert Sun School in Idyllwild and returned home to live with her parents at the Wilshire Comstock. A short while later, her sister

Sharon, who was attending the University of Southern California (USC) introduced Diane to a fellow student named Grant "Bud" Conroy.

In 1959, Grant had graduated Carmel High School in Northern California and was now studying business administration at USC and playing on the school's rugby team. At the time Diane and Grant were introduced, she was 17 years of age, and he was 24.

After spending time with Grant Conroy for several months, Diane believed she was pregnant. Left with either aborting the pregnancy or getting married, Diane and Grant secretly eloped in September 1966. Given that throughout the United States at that time, a minor under the age of 18 couldn't marry without parental consent, Diane and Grant either lied about her age or married outside the United States.

Six weeks later, Grant escorted Diane to the Coronet Debutante Ball that was held in Los Angeles on, according to Coronet tradition, the Saturday following Thanksgiving. Debutantes who are inducted into the Coronet Debutante Ball are the daughters of the upper-crust, well-connected before they reach college, and born into some of the world's wealthiest families.

Of course, being the daughter of Art Linkletter, Diane surely qualified. Besides her father's substantial wealth and influence, Diane's godfather was Disneyland's founder Walt Disney; her godmother was Academy Award winning actress Greer Garson; and Art was a close friend of actor Ronald Reagan, who would later become President of the United States. Photos taken that evening of Diane show her to be radiantly beautiful and the picture of robust health.

A short while after Diane attended the Debutante Ball, she discovered she wasn't pregnant. At some point, her father learned about her secret marriage and, using all his power and influence, immediately had the marriage annulled. As an aside, which will prove important in later chapters, throughout Diane's brief marriage to Grant Conroy, she lived at home with her parents.

Aside from our occasional phone calls or seeing each other around town, Diane and I continued on our separate journeys.

By the end of 1967, I had amassed enough units at SMCC to transfer to the University of California at Los Angeles (UCLA) where I elected to pursue a career in medicine. In addition to continuing to teach karate at Ed Parker's WLA school, I worked an assortment of part-time jobs, including selling men's clothes at the exclusive men's store Snyder & Son that was located inside the Century Plaza Hotel in Century City.

The fun and rewarding college life I enjoyed at SMCC turned out to be a small microcosm to what I encountered at UCLA, where I loved everything about campus life. Just to call myself a UCLA student was so exhilarating to me that going to class and getting excellent grades was a plus.

Although I initially was viewed as a conservative jock, after a while, I embraced some of the overtones of the hippie culture that pervaded the UCLA campus during the second half of the 1960s. Best of all, for the first time in my life I felt that I had a promising future because a four year college degree was within my grasp.

Around this same time, Diane was also making mammoth strides in her life. In the spring of 1968, she appeared on *The Red*

Skelton Show playing the role of Muggsy's daughter in the episode "Love Is an Itch You Can't Scratch." In that same episode, her father played the role of a hobo.

Then, after working summer stock, in July she toured US military bases throughout Europe and Vietnam with her father. Sometime in that same year, Diane and her father did a commercial together for "Circus Nuts" that today can be seen on YouTube.

Late that year, I happened to be at the "Santa Claus Lane Parade" down Hollywood Blvd. when a racecar suddenly came into view. Seated in the car and looking like a million dollars was Diane.

Finding my way to the end of the parade, I wrapped my arms around her and told her how great she looked. We talked for a while, and I said hello to her father, whom I hadn't seen in years.

To say that Diane was overjoyed and thrilled by the direction her life had taken would be a vast understatement. We both wished each other well and promised to stay in touch.

THREE

shoreham towers

In the fall of 1968, Diane left her parents' home at the Wilshire Comstock and moved into a sixth floor, one-bedroom apartment located at 8787 Shoreham Drive in West Hollywood, just off the Sunset Strip.

The apartment in the recently constructed Shoreham Towers was small (833 sq. ft.), although it included full service with concierge, pool, spa, sundeck, security, and valet parking. Generally speaking, the opulent Shoreham Towers was a downsized version of the Wilshire Comstock.

In the mid-1960s and 1970s, "The Strip" became a major gathering place for the counterculture and a haven for music groups. Bands such as Led Zeppelin, The Doors, The Byrds, Love, The Seeds, Frank Zappa, and many others played at clubs like the

Whisky a Go Go, the Roxy, Pandora's Box and the London Fog. In July 1965, Go-Go dancers also began performing.

Haight Ashbury and Woodstock were in full swing, and there was carefree laughter—and living—everywhere. This was the Sixties—Dr. Timothy Leary's call to "turn on, tune in, and drop out," coupled with Beatle mania, free love, and the constant hippie revolution against the escalating Vietnam War.

Although during that era sloppy, over-decorated "crash pads" were popular, Diane's apartment was neatly kept, tastefully decorated, and festooned with family pictures and a Steve Sachs psychedelic backlit poster that read FRODO PUFFS PIPE WEED. In 1968, Sachs was a pioneer in using fluorescent inks to produce psychedelic art in the hallucinogenic world of the 1960s. Attached to the outside of the front door was a handwritten sign that said:

To those of you entering, please give a minutes thought to the vibrations and feelings of which you brought with you. If they be of sound, sincere, and honest quality, do enter. On the other hand, be they different from those qualities listed above, do enter for I'll try to understand, signed Lady of the Manor, M. Diane L.

The décor of Diane's apartment shouldn't be taken as an indicator of her being a druggie. She was simply reflecting the era along with hundreds of thousands of other conservative youths throughout the country.

By way of example, at that same time, I was living in a small bachelor apartment close to UCLA that had the walls covered with paisley bedspreads and lit by several orange bug lights. I burned candles and incense, frequently wore love beads, and played Ravi Shankar music.

After five quarters at UCLA, I became disenchanted with college life. This was heightened when I took a job as an orderly at the UCLA hospital's emergency room. While there, several doctors told me that our country was verging on socialized medicine and that the glory days of being a highly paid, private physician were soon coming to an end.

Adding to this disillusionment, I was tired of being a broke college student who was constantly burdened with studying for midterms and finals. Coupled with my workload, I felt increasingly isolated, and I knew that graduate school would be far more demanding. Generally speaking, the novelty of college life was beginning to wear thin, and I was prone for a change.

In early 1969, Hollywood director Blake Edwards (best known for his Pink Panther films) walked into Ed Parker's WLA Kenpo Karate school with his ten-year-old son Geoffrey. At the time, I was teaching a private lesson, and soon learned from the school's manager that Blake was interested in hiring a karate teacher to come to his fiancee's home in Coldwater Canyon to teach private lessons to his young son.

In addition, Blake would be taking lessons when time permitted (Blake had been studying Kenpo with Ed Parker for a couple of years), as well as his Oscar-winning fiancée actress-singer Julie Andrews (best known for *The Sound of Music* and *Mary Poppins*).

Although initially I respectfully turned down Blake's offer because of my heavy schedule at work and school, he simply wouldn't take no for an answer. In the end, he offered me so much money that I finally accepted teaching him and his family on a trial basis.

Within the first month, Blake was so determined to keep me onboard that he gifted me with a new Jaguar XKE sports car (equipped with a phone), and asked that I stay with his wife Julie when he traveled out of the country to scout locations.

Then when summer arrived, Blake handed me the keys to his Malibu beach house where I was to write my first Hollywood screenplay (Blake was convinced that I had a writing talent). Over the next three months, I wrote my first screenplay while continuing to attend classes at UCLA.

After three months, I was forced to move out when Blake sold the house to actor Ryan O'Neal, who had become an overnight international superstar for his leading role in *Love Story*. Ryan eventually remodeled the house and lived in it with Farrah Fawcett and, in fact, still resides in that house today.

As if all those perks weren't enough, Blake told me that I'd be working on his next movie—a western called *Wild Rovers* for MGM starring Oscar-winner William Holden and Ryan O'Neal—that was to start principal photography in late October. Needless to say, by now I'd become smitten, if not seduced, by Hollywood and the people in it and quit my studies at UCLA. Ironically, if not serendipitously, my path and Diane's suddenly seemed to be heading toward a common road.

Although the luxurious apartment building that Diane moved to in West Hollywood—the Shoreham Towers—was a microcosm of the Wilshire Comstock, many of the neighboring apartment buildings were older were occupied by "street people" who frequented the Strip.

Understandably, Diane didn't relate well to many of the older, conservative professionals who could afford on their own to live in the upscale Shoreham Towers. She did, however, eventually connect with a group of people in the neighborhood, mainly those interested in the music business. Unfortunately, several of them had a checkered past.

Two such people lived in an apartment building directly across the street from the Shoreham Towers at 1211 Horn Avenue, and both were highly connected to the drug culture and seasoned street people of the Strip.

One was a struggling musician named Robert Parker McDonald, aka Bobby Jameson, who was three years older than Diane and making increasing use of LSD, as well as other drugs and alcohol. Frustrated and disillusioned that he had never received any financial rewards for his music, over the course of several years, Bobby Jameson had been arrested 27 times, including assaulting a police officer. He was hospitalized on more than one occasion after drug overdoses and suicide attempts, and had actually been pronounced dead on two occasions.

Jameson definitely lived life on the edge. He was a prime example of a person who in later life could attest to the validity of the old quip about the Sixties: "If you can remember them, you weren't there!"

At the outset, I'd like to make clear that although Bobby Jameson had led a troubled early life battling several formidable demons, in later years he completely turned his life around and became a hardworking, honest citizen and a valued friend to many. Throughout my conversations I had with him, I found him to be a sincere person who truly cared for Diane and was in all likelihood a positive influence in her life. I have no doubt that Diane always considered Bobby Jameson a friend who had her best interests at heart.

Sharing the apartment with Jameson was Edward "Ed" Durston, who was six years older than Diane and had a shady past and a bad reputation as a self-absorbed person who used people and wasn't to be trusted. At the time Diane met Bobby Jameson and Ed Durston, Jameson's beautiful girlfriend Nancy Harwood was also living in the apartment and had recently been featured as a "Playmate of the Month" in Hugh Hefner's *Playboy* magazine. As an aside, their apartment had been sublet from Timothy Rooney, son of actor Mickey Rooney.

Although Diane knew these people, from all that I've been able to discern, she only minimally interacted with them. Besides having enrolled in a few college courses, Diane's main focus remained on her acting career.

In an interview she granted around that time to a popular columnist, she proudly said that she had no intention of disowning the name Linkletter or the help it could give her. "I've had my mind set on being an actress since I was eight," she said, "and I find doors don't open too easily in this business. I'm delighted that my name is Linkletter. I make a point to take every possible advantage of the fact that I am a member of that family. I'm a very lucky girl."

There was another reason why she was glad for any help

that her father could provide her. "I love the guy," she beamed, "and he gets such a big kick out of my movie and TV activities. He wants to know everything that I'm doing. He makes sure I have the right photographer. He checks over my stills to see that none is released that will prove unflattering. I certainly wouldn't deprive him of those pleasures by telling him I didn't want his help."

From time to time, Diane had a way of attracting, and letting, the wrong people into her life, which happened around September of 1968 when she met Harvey Dareff, who was seven years her senior.

As was the case with other struggling opportunists, Dareff dabbled on the fringes of Hollywood's entertainment business, hoping to find an open door or one he could kick open. After dating Diane for a short while, in April of 1969, Dareff moved in with Diane and, according to a subsequent police report, was essentially supported by her.

Like Bobby Jameson and Ed Durston, Harvey Dareff was well known to law enforcement. According to police records, undercover investigators had been watching Dareff for some time and had identified him, along with Jameson and Durston, as a drug dealer. In a separate investigation, Dareff and Durston were also labeled as car thieves.

The most alarming police investigation of Harvey Dareff, however, had to do with the highly publicized Manson murders of Sharon Tate and others in early August 1969. According to investigators, they had information that Harvey F. Dareff may have gone to the director Roman Polanski's residence on Cielo

Drive on the evening of the murders to possibly buy or sell some form of narcotics.

Diane was aware of her father keeping a watchful eye on her, and at times welcomed his concerns, while at other times felt he was meddling, which was a typical teenage reaction.

When word of Dareff's police record got back to Diane's father, along with reports that Diane and Dareff were constantly arguing, Art made a bold move to get Dareff out of Diane's life. According to Bobby Jameson, one afternoon, Art Linkletter met privately with Harvey Dareff and offered him a check for $10,000 (in 2016 its value would be $66,000) and told him to take the money and agree to stay away from Diane.

According to Jameson, Dareff turned down Art's check. Perhaps Harvey should have taken the money because over the next several months his heated feuding with Diane escalated. When it finally reached the breaking point in the third week of September, Harvey Dareff packed his bags and traveled 3,000 miles to New York, allegedly never to see or speak to Diane again.

Diane took the breakup with Harvey Dareff in stride and continued to focus on her college studies and her acting career. It was around this time that she and her father made a 45 rpm record entitled "We Love You, Call Collect" that the following year won a Grammy for Best Spoken Word Recording in 1969. In addition, they made a commercial together for "Circus Nuts" that can be seen on YouTube. On that video, Diane looks healthy and happy, and it's clear they have a wonderful rapport.

Now that Harvey Dareff was gone from Diane's life, Diane resumed casual dating. On Friday evening, October 3, 1969, she went out with a friend named Robert Reitman, who was much closer to her age. Robert was a gifted athlete and had done well in school, and was at the time working for the Walt Disney Record Company that distributed "We Love You, Call Collect."

That night, they attended the spectacular celestial show at Griffith Park Observatory's 290-seat planetarium theater that was popular with the youth. Around midnight, Robert dropped Diane back at her apartment and bid her goodnight. A short while later, Diane joined a street party that was taking place near the Shoreham Towers and went late into the night.

FOUR

october 4, 1969

The following morning shortly after 9 a.m., emergency vehicles were converging on the Shoreham Towers where a crowd of onlookers and members of the media had gathered outside. Across the street, Ed Durston was holed up in his apartment and was soon joined by a flustered Bobby Jameson, who asked Durston what the hell had happened.

According to Durston, he and Diane were sitting in her living room, talking for half the night about life, and everything was okay. Then seemingly out of the blue, Diane started acting crazy. "She suddenly got up and went out on the balcony," Durston told Jameson, "and started climbing on the railing like she was gonna jump off."

Durston then claimed to have run to the balcony and drug her off the railing and pulled her back into the living room where he pinned her to the floor and said, "What the fuck are you doing, Diane? What the fuck is wrong with you?"

Jameson recalled that Durston was tightly wringing his hands as if trying to get them clean. "I pleaded with her to tell me what was wrong," Durston continued, according to Jameson. "She told me she was just screwing around and that everything was okay and to let her up because it was just a joke."

Durston stated that he made Diane promise that if he let her up, she wouldn't do anything crazy. "I let her up," Durston said to Jameson, "and she said she was going to go in the kitchen and get a glass of water, and I said okay. She then walked into the kitchen, and I turned around to watch her and she just climbed up on the countertop by the window over the sink. I ran into the kitchen and tried to grab her, but she just went out the window before I could get there." After pausing for a moment to, according to Jameson, summon up enough courage, Durston said, "I had a hold of her ankle, man, I had her by the ankle, but I couldn't hold her, I just couldn't hold her, man."

There were two other people who witnessed Diane's fall. One was a neighbor, Dick Shephard, who lived across the street and was looking out his bay window and saw Diane in the air, heard a scream, and watched in horror as she fell six floors and hit the sidewalk.

The second person was Jimmy George, who lived below the apartment where Durston and Jameson lived with Jameson's girlfriend Nancy Harwood. Jimmy had been standing across the street from the Shoreham Towers and saw Diane falling to the ground below. Hours later, he related the following to Jameson.

At first, Jimmy thought someone was playing a practical joke and had thrown something out the window, but then realized it was a person. He didn't know at first that it was Diane, and he'd seen her hit the ground. He was in shock, but ran over to where the body had landed, and that was when he realized it was Diane. He told Jameson that he couldn't do anything for her, and it made him feel like an asshole. He said she was still alive when he reached her, and that she looked up at him but couldn't speak. He said she was bleeding a lot from her head, and he wanted to help her, but didn't know what to do.

Jameson later stated that Jimmy was always a happy-go-lucky guy, but on that day he was broken. It was the last time Jameson ever saw Jimmy, and he often wondered how the experience had altered Jimmy's life.

Diane was taken by ambulance first to Hollywood Receiving Hospital, and then to the University of Southern California Medical Center on State Street. She was pronounced dead on arrival, just two weeks short of her 21st birthday.

Diane had no way of knowing that at 9 a.m. on October 4, 1969 her death was destined to become a focal point of a sweeping anti-drug movement in America.

Before an autopsy had been performed, her father claimed to the media that he had learned that Diane had taken LSD the night before her death. Art Linkletter was quoted as saying, "It isn't suicide because she wasn't herself. She was murdered by the people who manufacture and sell LSD."

Rather than hide from the press, Art went public with a vehement anti-drug campaign, stating that on the day that Diane had taken "a much stronger dose of this poison than she should have" and focused his anger on Dr. Timothy Leary, the drug advocate and former educator, but also blamed the companies that manufacture LSD.

Art Linkletter, understandably devastated, became one of the most vocal critics of the drug counterculture, forcefully speaking out against drugs at every opportunity, while telling the grin tale of his daughter's LSD death. Dr. Leary, the LSD guru who had urged young people to "turn on, tune in, and drop out," became Art Linkletter's archenemy.

FIVE

the investigation

Within the hour sheriff's homicide investigators converged on Diane's apartment. Initially, they stood in the hallway and noted the burnt parchment type paper attached to the door that read in long hand the message to those entering and signed by "Lady of the Manner, M. Diane L."

They then opened the door to a small hall that led to the main living room where they noted a couch, and on both sides of the couch wooden tables with large lamps. They also noted the adjacent balcony and sliding glass door. On the southwest wall was a large round cabinet, on top of which was a radio record player combination. The radio was on and was tuned to 92 FM.

On the wall were two paintings and an area covered with psychedelic type posters; one of which read FRODO PUFFS PIPE WEED.

In the northwest corner of the living room was a table with numerous articles on it. Starting from the east side of the table was a book titled *The Story of O* by Pauline Reage; a half-consumed bottle of soda pop containing a brown liquid; a note written with red ink on a 5" by 8" piece of paper, which stated, "I remember singing on a silver day, I remember loving you in a golden way, Did a lot of talking I shouldn't ought done, Had a lot of power then, I was number one. I remember leaving you, a thing I still regret, as I drink my coffee and smoke my cigarette."

Another book was on the table, *Wisdom of Soul* by Randolph Stevens, and a checkbook with a golden cover on top of the book and a blue with yellow metal trim purse next to it. There was a glass containing a clear liquid resembling water. On the far west end of the table was a stack of numerous papers.

On the northwest end of the living room was the entrance to the kitchen. On the west side of the kitchen, starting from the south, was an oven, a stove, and a drain board, which is approximately 26" wide and 5' long. This area is covered with yellow tile. On the tiled area was a white with brown trim plate containing cookie crumbs. Scattered about the plate were two full cookies and more crumbs. There was also a yellow cookie jar and small plastic flowers. There was also a small piece of paper with the name Ruben Guverra, #656-4483.

The investigator continued taking notes: Above the drain board is a window which is 45" high and 38-1/2" wide. The north side of the window was open and it left an open area of 15-3/8" by 45". It should be noted that there was no screen on the window. There were beige drapes, and at the time of measurement, the ones to the north half were protruding. It should also be noted that this drain board area is 37-1/2" from the kitchen floor and the window is 6" above the drain board. On the north end of the kitchen is a sink. On the east end was a refrigerator. On top of the refrigerator is a lamp shade with beads around it and a red bulb.

The bathroom is on the northeast end of the apartment. It has two wash basins on the north side. There was a partially smoked cigarette resembling tobacco which appeared to have been burning and consumed itself, on the eastern most basin. It should be noted that the light in the bathroom was on.

On the southeast portion of the apartment was the bedroom. On the north end of the bedroom was a Singer sewing machine, on which were two dresses. The thread on the machine was the same color as one of the dresses. There was a Norelco tape recorder on the northeast corner, next to a waste paper basket. The headboard of the bed was against the east wall at the midpoint. On both sides of the bed were night tables.

On the north table was a book entitled *The Godfather* by Mario Puzo, open and facing down. Two more books were closed: *The Naked Ape* and *Linkletter Downunder* (Hardcover 1968, Prentice Hall, Linkletter in Australia). Car keys were in a key holder similar to a "roach holder," which is commonly used to hold partially consumed marijuana cigarettes. Framed picture of Diane and Art. Prescription for Codeine and Ephedrine. Four cards: Lassers,

Columbus, Ohio and written in ink on it was "Diane, who has principles, ideals, and a marvelous person, have an easy trip." Robert D. Wood, President of CBS Television network. Third from Herbert Sorwin, Veterans Administration Center. Fourth written in ink, "Sometimes I forget how much you mean to me, Love, H." The investigators noted that throughout the house, everything appeared to be in order and there were no obvious signs of a struggle.

When the investigators learned that Diane Linkletter had been in the company of Edward Durston during the early morning hours prior to her death, they had Durston brought into the station for questioning.

Fortunately for Durston, the investigators knew nothing about what Durston had told Bobby Jameson hours earlier because Durston gave the investigators a substantially different accounting of what had transpired in Diane's apartment. Had the investigators known the details of the accounting Durston had made to Bobby Jameson, Durston would have had considerable explaining to do.

According to the official police records, Durston told the investigators that on the day prior to Diane's death, Diane stated to him that she was going out and she requested that he come to her apartment after she came home from her date with Robert Reitman. When she arrived home around midnight, Diane came to his apartment on Horn Avenue and asked him to come to her apartment around 3 a.m. and that she was going to bake some cookies.

At the beginning of the interview, Durston stated that Diane had dropped some acid and that they talked for several hours. Further, that Diane had indicated she was despondent, and they went to the balcony of her apartment and looked out over the city. Durston went on to state that the can of soda that the investigators had asked him about earlier that was on the table was being consumed by him, and that the glass of water that was also on the table was being consumed by Diane.

Durston stated that sometime around daybreak, he and Diane again went to the balcony and, below at the main entrance, saw an apartment house attendant named Scottie walking his Saint Bernard dog. The leash came off the dog and the dog began to run away. Scottie threw the leash at the dog and began to run after it. When Diane saw this, she became horrified and advised Durston that Scottie was going to kill his dog.

Shortly after, they returned to the inside of the apartment and Diane became hysterical, causing Durston to try to physically restrain her. Also, at this time he called Diane's brother Robert and told him that Diane had dropped acid. Durston also talked to [redacted] and Bob apparently advised that he would be over as soon as possible. When Robert Linkletter was contacted, he stated that he did receive a phone call from Diane and that he did advise Durston and Diane that he was coming over.

Durston went on to tell investigators that after the phone call, he and Diane went to the bedroom and sat on the bed, and that Diane was now calm and composed. She then got up and left the bedroom and entered the hall, walked across the living room with him following her. She then proceeded into the kitchen, climbed up on the drain board, and proceeded out of the window.

At this time, Durston reached Diane and attempted to grab her belt at her back and also attempted to reach her through the drapes, but he was unable to stop her from going through the window. He stated that in his left hand he grabbed a handful of drapes. He stated that he then called the police and proceeded to the lobby of Shoreham Towers where he advised the switchboard operator to call the police. He then went outside and the police came.

The police had reason to be concerned about Diane having spent the last six hours of her life with Ed Durston. Besides being a suspected drug dealer and car thief, Durston, along with Harvey Dareff, was a suspect in the Manson killings that had occurred two months earlier at the home of Sharon Tate's husband, director Roman Polanski.

With their concerns mounting, the investigators asked Durston if he was willing to take a polygraph test, to which he agreed. As stated in the police report, the list of questions the investigators asked Durston are as follows:

Have you told the complete truth in this case?
Do you know if Diane jumped from the window?
Did you push Diane from the window?
Were you alone with Diane when she met her death?
Did you have a fight with Diane just prior to her death?
Have you ever caused anyone's death?
Other than what you told me, have you ever been present at anyone's death?
Do you now own a gun?

Have you ever owned a pistol?
Did you lie to the investigating officers?
Are you withholding any information about this case?
Did you cause Diane's death?
Have you sold any narcotics within the past three months?
Have you sold any narcotics within the past three weeks?
Have you taken any narcotics in the past 24 hours?

Upon completing the test—the results of which were pending and subsequently never listed in any report available to the public—Durston claimed he was exhausted, and was put up in a motel that was paid for by the West Hollywood Sheriff's Office. The following day, he was given a second polygraph test, after which he traveled to Lovelock, Nevada to stay with his parents.

Diane's body was fast tracked to autopsy at 3 p.m. that same day. Initially, upon a precursory examination of the body, the Chief Medical Examiner stated that Diane had died from cerebral contusions, extensive, massive skull fracture, and multiple fractures of her extremities. In addition, he noted a rather extensive laceration-contusion of her upper lip, that her anterior chest showed a faint outline of a brassiere, and her right wrist showed an extensive contusion, although there was no palpable fracture. After further noting that the lab tests showed that Diane's body was totally absent of any drugs and alcohol, the medical examiner changed the mode of death to "suicide."

When the autopsy showed no signs of drugs in her system, Art Linkletter changed his story, claiming that Diane had suffered an LSD flashback from months earlier, which had caused her to jump out the window (worth noting is that LSD is a powerful drug and it takes an extremely small amount to affect the user. As such, it generally will not be detected in tests, especially those used in 1969).

The media, of course, ran with the story, and used Art Linkletter's claims to create the narrative, without doing much investigating of their own. By the time the dust had settled, the story had been transformed in the minds of most people to reflect an old urban legend about a girl, high on LSD, who jumped out her window because she thought she could fly.

Over time, word began to circulate (eventually finding its way onto the Internet) that Diane was into heroin since she was 13 or 14 and had mentioned suicide on several occasions—and supposedly had recently used LSD three or four times a week. Those who had been close to Diane, particularly her early childhood and school friends, vehemently denied these allegations.

Without question, I found the notion of Diane having been a serious drug abuser dating back to her adolescent years to be totally preposterous. As I had anticipated, I discovered the initial source of these claims on the sheriff investigator's report that I obtained through the Freedom of Information Act (County of Los Angeles – Sheriff's Department – Supplementary Report, File No. 069-07789-0978-491, Active Investigation Coroner's Case #69-10931).

SIX

interrogation of grant conroy

On the day following Diane's death, Homicide Investigator Lt. Norman Hamilton of the West Hollywood Sheriff's Department interviewed Grant Conroy, who at the time gave his address as 2430 Benedict Canyon, and phone number as 827-6100.

Conroy stated that he was married to Diane when she was 17 years of age and that the marriage was annulled, stating further that he and Diane got married because Diane thought she was pregnant.

Conroy stated that during the marriage Diane used narcotics and all dangerous drugs and that he attempted to stop her from using these chemicals and was somewhat successful.

He further stated that during the last year, he had seen Diane two or three times, the last time being two weeks prior to the incident. Conroy went on to tell Hamilton that Diane had been using heroin and dangerous drugs since she was 13 or 14 years old.

Moreover, during her enrollment at Desert Sun, she had been using marijuana, and during the time she attended college in San Diego, she was also using drugs. Diane attended various schools during the marriage and during the last six months of the marriage, she had used speed, and then methedrine (a brand of methamphetamine). He stated that she mentioned suicide on several occasions. Further, Conroy claimed that Diane used LSD three or four times a week.

Without any doubt, I found Grant Conroy's statements to Investigator Hamilton to be totally absurd. The picture of Diane that Conroy painted wasn't even remotely close to the Diane I knew—or anyone else I knew and/or had spoken to.

Of all of Conroy's statements, the idea that Diane was using heroin in the early 1960s was outrageous. Where in the world would she have gotten heroin and "other dangerous drugs" while living at home with her parents and four siblings? No one I knew in the early 1960s had even heard of heroin except for perhaps the 1955 movie *The Man With the Golden Arm* starring Frank Sinatra that was about a strung out junkie. In fact, marijuana didn't become known to our country's mainstream youth until the arrival of The Beatles and the British music invasion that began in the mid-1960s.

Moreover, Conroy's claim that Diane was using speed and LSD during the marriage made no sense whatsoever, given that during the entire time Diane was married to Conroy, she lived at home with her parents. As such, I can't imagine how she could have been using these drugs on a regular basis without her parents becoming aware of this.

Wanting to talk personally with Grant Conroy, I found him on social media and reached out to him via email. After a brief overview of my relationship to Diane and her family when Diane and I were teenagers, I left the door open for Conroy to give me a *Reader's Digest* version of his personal relationship with Diane.

What I got, instead, was a long-winded dissertation. According to Conroy, from the moment they met, he and Diane had been inseparable for two years and had eventually eloped. In addition, Conroy stated that he was welcomed into Diane's family with open arms and had, in fact, traveled with the family extensively during the summer to the High Sierras and that he often traveled on Diane's brother Jack Linkletter's Beechcraft airplane.

I didn't receive one email of this nature. I received several. And I wasn't the only one. It turned out that Scott Michaels, who put together the popular website "Find A Grave" had also received a barrage of emails from Grant Conroy that were filled with much of the same "close family ties" between Grant Conroy and the Linkletter family.

Of course, what soon jumped at me was the obvious question as to why Art Linkletter, if Grant Conroy was the son-in-law from heaven, went to such great lengths to use his power and influence to have Diane's marriage to Conroy annulled.

In sharp contrast, it would seem to me that when Diane's father learned of his daughter's elopement (Diane had turned 18 by this time), that he would have been overjoyed and wanted to make his daughter's marriage legal. If Diane's parents were so thrilled with Diane's husband, they would have publicly announced their daughter's engagement with great fanfare and planned an elaborate wedding (both Diane's sisters, Dawn and Sharon, were married when they were 20 years of age). But, of course, this isn't what happened—and any clear thinking person would be led to ask why.

After Conroy established that he was the best of friends with the Linkletter family, further stating that he had years of loving letters from Diane stored in a safe and always wanted the best for his beloved former wife, I asked him why he made what I felt were patently false and disparaging comments to the sheriff homicide investigators about Diane being a serious drug addict and that her abuse went as far back as to when she was 13 years old.

Conroy's response was dramatically different from what he told law enforcement. "I've never witnessed any drugs of any kind around Diane Linkletter," Conroy fired back. This was followed by his claim that I was making all this up, and that he'd never been interviewed by anyone from the sheriff's, which he later changed to when he heard about Diane's death, he was living in Northern California in Carmel and that he traveled to Los Angeles the next day to offer whatever information he could to investigators and because he wanted to know what happened.

That said, however, he wanted to be clear that he was never "technically interviewed." When I told him that the sheriff's report mentioned that there was a stenographer present when he was questioned at length by Investigator Hamilton, Conroy denied this was the case, further stating that he had a witness who would collaborate his story that no record was made of his brief discussion with Hamilton.

"I never was shown the police report you're speaking about by a detective Hamilton or I would have contradicted it ASAP," Conroy wrote back, further stating that Hamilton had quickly dismissed him, which, under the circumstances surprised Conroy. "I spoke for maybe four or five minutes," Conroy offered, adding that Hamilton had no interest in an old boyfriend of Diane's, which seemed to be Hamilton's mindset.

Although Conroy told Hamilton that during the last year, he'd seen Diane two or three times, the last time being two weeks prior to the incident, Conroy said to me in an email, as well as Scott Michaels of the Findadeath website, that he was doing film work in Europe and hadn't seen Diane for the past two years and that he regretted not being around for her if needed, although he claimed to have talked a couple of times with Diane by telephone.

From everything I've been able to discern, from the time Grant Conroy left for Europe two years before Diane's death, they never saw or spoke with each other again.

Days later, Conroy emailed me again, claiming that he had no idea where I had gotten my information, but probably from some tabloid. Again, he claimed to have never witnessed any use of any questionable substances during his relationship with Diane, stating further that he didn't believe Diane had any problems later, as she was "well-disciplined and precocious, very popular, and a leader, and was very close to her mother Lois."

Again referencing his stash of vaulted love letters from Diane, he assured me that any mention of an illegal substance, or even a reference to that subject, is not in any of these letters and that he was completely unaware of anything having changed in her life that would have led to her becoming a drug addict.

No matter how much Conroy proclaimed otherwise, I kept reminding him that the statements I was referring to that he made about Diane's drug use were contained in an official investigation report that is a matter of public record. After not hearing from Conroy for a few days, he resurfaced with a new twist, no doubt after considerable thought.

Once again, I received yet another email from Conroy that brought to mind William Shakespear's quote "Methinks thou dost protest too much!" In this latest offering, Conroy reiterated that he had never expressed the fabricated story that I stated he made to a police investigator in the investigator's "alleged" police report about Diane's "alleged" suicide just before her 21st birthday. Then ironically, he added "If you would be so kind, please send me a copy of that report."

Conroy assured me that if the report stated what I said it did, then Diane's death took on a new issue, specifically that a "false report" by a homicide investigator would indicate some kind of collusion. According to Conroy, considering the high profile that Diane's death had taken on, coupled with "Art's persona," that this indicated that either Art Linkletter or "others" might be involved in creating a false biography and associating this with Diane's death.

After dropping what had the appearance of a red herring, Conroy again stated that he never made those statements to investigators that were being attributed to him. "I would never have done that," he emphasized. "I cared for Diane very deeply, and she was the all American girl that reminded everybody greatly of Shirley Temple. Drugs were not a part of her youth when I knew her. Send me that 'alleged' report. I look forward to straightening the record regarding this wonderful young woman."

What a major distraction. Or was it? Considering the capricious nature of Conroy's story, I was hesitant to believe anything he said. In any event, he now wanted me to consider that members of the West Hollywood Sheriff's Department fabricated their investigation reports into a "false biography," and that they did so because they were in collusion with either Diane's father or "others."

Later expanding on this new theory, Conroy felt that one of these other people may have been filmmaker John Waters, who within a week of Diane's death made a cheesy nine-minute exploitation film called *The Diane Linkletter Story*.

In the film, actors playing the parts of Mr. and Mrs. Linkletter fret about Diane's recent behavior, which includes taking drugs and dating a lowlife named Jim. Eventually, the parents confront Diane, which results in her suicide under the influence of LSD.

Waters later claimed that the film was "accidental" and that he and his friends had improvised a story while testing a new synch-sound camera (later used on *Multiple Maniacs*) and that the film was never meant to be seen by the public. In this tasteless film, Diane was played by Divine, a highly shocking and entertaining transvestite heralded as the international icon of bad taste cinema. As a footnote, the film was unreleased in any form until it showed up on a 1990 videotape entitled *A Divine Double Feature*.

Conroy wasted no time jumping on this diversion and portrayed John Waters' short film as being an attempt to exploit himself off a tragic incident and Art Linkletter's "self-assumptions," pointing out that because of Diane's alleged suicide, Art's stellar career had waned, which Conroy felt might have been the motivation behind this false tabloid aftermath.

"Two stories come to mind that contributed greatly to the large press 'misinformation' that tagged her as having drug problems," Conroy offered. "John Water's short 'fiction' film *THE DIANE LINKLETTER STORY* and Scott Michaels' of "FIND A GRAVE" derogatory biography (possibly copying the theme of Waters' film) which was picked up on the Internet and closely associated with Diane's name and cause of death—and falsely fabricated statements stated to be mine."

Then in summation, Conroy conveyed that he suspected all these years that this entire business about Diane taking LSD and being the victim of the drug culture had something to do with Art Linkletter's power and influence.

According to Conroy, Diane's father was the official master

of ceremonies for the Old Hollywood A-list (on the Republican side especially) and that Diane's death being ruled a suicide almost destroyed him, except for "his great wit and stature."

Conroy theorized that the LSD story saved Art Linkletter's reputation somewhat, even though his long running TV show was ultimately cancelled shortly thereafter. Conroy further pointed out that the behaviors of Hollywood's cops have often come under suspicion and that the John Waters film was "too quickly timed," convenient and seedy, thus lending additional suspicion to the entire ugly matter.

Was Conroy suggesting that Art Linkletter helped fabricate, if not singlehandedly orchestrated, the entire LSD story, which meant that his son Robert lied about the nature of the phone call he claimed to have received from Diane in order to save his father's reputation as a model loving father figure that had for decades been a major pillar of his public image?

If true, then this would mean that Art Linkletter threw his daughter's reputation under the bus. And if Grant Conroy's theory has any truth to it, then these statements about Diane's longstanding drug use that Conroy made to the sheriff investigators, if untrue, were either fabricated by the investigators—thus framing Conroy—or made by Conroy at the behest of Diane's father or "others."

In my view, this entire scenario put forth by Conroy amounts to a monumental stretch and has the overtone of fundamentally acting as a major diversion from the essential elements of Hamilton's investigation.

When I stated this opinion to Conroy, he held firm, most

likely because he had dug himself into a hole and decided to get nasty. "Your professional career must be struggling," he said accusingly, "to try and sell a story about teenage love a half century ago using a famous name to make it happen. You have my sympathy."

And then he elected to extend a stern warning. "Tell your associates they're opening a can of worms on a much bigger, well-detailed story where prudent discretion is wise. I suggest you let sleeping dogs lie. Sid Korshak would concur."

For those readers who are unfamiliar with Sid Korshak, he was a lawyer for the Chicago mafia and considered the mob's main man in Los Angeles. Sidney Korshak's law practice brought him in contact with many mobsters, such as Al Capone, Frank Nitti, Sam Giancana, Tony Accardo and Moe Dalitz. His services were used by the upper ranks of both legitimate and illegitimate business in the US.

Why Conroy felt it necessary to mention Sidney Korshak to me is anyone's guess. I wrote back to Conroy telling him that a mafia lawyer who has been dead for 20 years has nothing to do with the derogatory comments Conroy told the sheriff's investigators about Diane, and that if his intention was to intimidate me with inserting this mob attorney into the conversation, his ploy failed miserably.

Arguably, there are a handful of ways that one can interpret what took place during the meeting between Grant Conroy and Lt. Hamilton on the day following Diane's death, specifically with regards to the truth of Conroy's statements and the imagined motivations of Art Linkletter with regard to whether he was in collusion with law enforcement, filmmaker John Waters, and/or "others."

Although I ascribe little, if any, credibility to Grant Conroy's theory that Diane's father had anything to do with creating a false narrative about Diane's death in order to rehabilitate his weakening public image, I have tremendous compassion for what Art Linkletter and his wife had to be going through.

Although there may be some truth that Art attempted to blur the line between Diane's tragic death and what may have caused it, one can only speculate as to his motivation for doing so. Worth noting is that it has never been uncommon for friends and family who are left behind after a loved one takes their own life to diligently work to convince others that the death was caused by something other than a deliberate ending of a life.

Sorryfully. only three months earlier, Art Linkletter's son-in-law, John Zweyer, who was married to Art and Lois's eldest daughter Dawn, committed suicide because he was distraught over his failing insurance business.

In the view of countless thousands throughout the world, and spanning many generations, Art Linkletter was a champion of family values, a pillar of his community, and a devoted and loving father and husband. Even prior to his daughter's death, Art Linkletter was vitally concerned with what he saw as the eroding state of family values, and he was actively engaged in lecturing across the country on the chosen topic of "Permissiveness in this Society." (Indeed, he'd been in Colorado to deliver such a talk at the time of Diane's death.)

At the time of Art Linkletter's death in 2010 at the age of 97, he and Lois were coming up on their 76th wedding anniversary. The longevity of their marriage that survived all those years in Hollywood without a single scandal, was, and still is, by all accounts a rarity in the entertainment business.

In conclusion, this chapter specifically addressed Grant Conroy's comment to law enforcement that have, for the past 45 years, been the official source behind the notion that Diane had a serious drug problem dating back to her early teen years.

According to Conroy's own words recently made to me, the statements contained in the decades-old sheriff investigator's report regarding Diane's alleged drug use and are attributed to Grant Conroy (1) are patently false, and (2) were never made by him.

As such, it is reasonable to forever dispense with the false perception that Diane Linkletter ever in her lifetime had a serious drug problem and, secondly, that this in turn brings into question whether or not she took LSD on the night before she fell from her sixth floor apartment.

And if LDS wasn't the cause of her panicked hysteria that ultimately led to her death, as implied by Ed Durston, then what was?

SEVEN

*october 4, 1969
revisited, part 1*

In order to arrive at a better understanding of how and why Diane died, it's important to make a step-by-step analysis of the key elements surrounding her death, paying strict attention to inconsistencies, false statements and innuendo, and omissions.

First, we should examine Diane's mental state and movements prior to Ed Durston arriving at her apartment at 3 a.m. Diane had broken up with Harvey Dareff only a few weeks ago and was again going out with male friends and perhaps potential boyfriends. From all appearances, she was in good spirits throughout her evening with Robert Reitman at the Griffith Park Observatory, and also enjoyed herself at the street party that, according to Bobby Jameson, went into the wee hours of the morning.

One of many curious aspects of Durston's accounting to

Investigator Hamilton is his statement that upon returning from her date around midnight, Diane went to his apartment and asked him to join her at her apartment in three hours because she was going to bake cookies.

Does this mean that at midnight, Ed Durston wasn't at the street party, as were Bobby Jameson, Diane, and most likely many of their friends? Are we also supposed to believe that at midnight Diane was a crystal ball of sorts and predicted that she'd stay at the party for three hours and then return alone to her apartment to bake cookies? Why not one a.m. or two a.m. or maybe not until daybreak? Why would Durston make a point of telling this to Hamilton?

In my view, Durston specifically told the investigator this (note that Durston never mentioned this to Bobby Jameson) because he was trying to establish the idea that he had personally been invited to Diane's apartment by her; and if that were true, then the two of them were friends; at least, given that she hadn't invited anyone else over at three in the morning for cookies.

In my view, it's far more reasonable to assume that Diane stayed at the street party for a couple of hours, and then around two-thirty in the morning when the party was breaking up, returned (with or without Durston) to her apartment—and shortly after arriving decided to bake some cookies.

According to what Durston told the police, he arrived at Diane's apartment around 3 a.m. The question, however, is did he come to her apartment on the spur of the moment, invited or uninvited? Surely, he was known to the 24-hour doorman who acted as security and most likely would have passed Durston through, had Durston been alone. And Durston would have known that Diane was awake because he would have seen her leave the street party (assuming Durston was actually present) or been able to see the lights on in her apartment from his apartment across the street.

My point is that I find curious Durston's comments to the investigators that Diane had hours earlier invited him to come to her apartment. It just seemed forced.

As an aside, knowing Diane as I did—and Bobby Jameson would concur with this—had Ed Durston appeared at her apartment uninvited at three in the morning, Diane would have graciously allowed him to come in, at least for a while. She was just that way—polite and practically incapable of turning a friend, and even an acquaintance, away. Moreover, I believe it makes more sense that Diane never intended to bake cookies at three in the morning, but offered to do so when Durston arrived, either unexpectedly or because he escorted her back to her apartment when the street party ended.

One aspect of the investigator's report that jumped out at me was the a copy of the book *The Story of O* by Pauline Reage that was found in Diane's living room. For those readers who are unfamiliar with this book, it is the story of a young, beautiful fashion photographer in Paris. One day her lover, Rene, takes her to a chateau, where she is enslaved, with Rene's approval, and systematically sexually assaulted by various other men. Later, Rene turns the woman over to Sir Stephen, an English friend who intensifies the brutality. The book was initially published in Paris, France in 1954, but appeared in the United States in 1965 when it was published by Ballantine Books. Over the years, *The Story of O* has been read by tens of thousands of people in the BDSM subculture, which stands for bondage, discipline (or domination), sadism, and masochism.

Without question, this would be the last book I would have expected to find in Diane's possession. To illustrate my point, *The Story of O* is in sharp contrast to the other books found in Diane's apartment—*Wisdom of Soul, The Godfather, The Naked Ape,* and *Linkletter Downunder.*

I have no question that what has been known as standard reading in the BDSM community did not belong to Diane. And if that's true, then how did this book end up in her apartment? Who brought it there? And why? Was it a mere coincidence that this book was sitting on the same table as Ed Durston's can of soda?

Next, I think it would be instructive to review the two different stories that Durston told to Bobby Jameson and the police. In the first version that was told to Bobby Jameson, Durston claimed that: (1) He and Diane are sitting in the living room talking casually when out of the blue, Diane ran onto the balcony and started climbing over the railing, (2) Durston ran to her and stopped her from jumping over the rail, then pulled her back into the living room where he pinned her to the floor, (3) when Diane claimed she had been joking and promised not to do anything crazy, Durston let her go, at which time (4) Diane ran to the kitchen and jumped out the window, and (5) Durston got a hold of her ankle but couldn't hold her and she fell to her death.

The above is substantially different from the accounting

Durston gave the sheriff's investigators only a few hours later, as follows: (1) When around midnight Diane returned from her date with Robert Reitman, she went to Durston's apartment and asked him to come to her apartment at 3 a.m. and that she planned on baking cookies, (2) that Diane had dropped acid, and that he and Diane talked for several hours, (3) they walked out onto her balcony and looked out over the city, returned to the living room, and then around daybreak again walked out to the balcony, at which time Diane became horrified when she believed the doorman named Scottie was going to kill his St. Bernard dog, (4) Durston and Diane return to the living room where Diane continued to be hysterical, causing Durston to physically restrain her, (5) at this time, Durston stated that he called Diane's brother Robert and told him that Diane had taken acid. Robert said he would come right over, (6) Durston and Diane then went to the bedroom and sat on her bed, at which time Diane became calm and composed, (7) Diane then got up, walked through the living room and into the kitchen, with Durston following her, (8) arriving in the kitchen, Diane climbed onto the counter and went out the window, (9) Durston tried to grab her, but was only able to grab a handful of drapes, and (10) moments after Diane fell to her death, Durston called the police.

There are several key discrepancies in these two versions. In Durston's first recollection—the one he tells Bobby Jameson—he fails to mention that Diane took acid. In my view, Durston didn't mention this because Jameson would have asked why Diane took acid and where did she get it? In the discussions I had with Bobby Jameson, he never mentioned that Diane used LSD. The only two sources of this critical claim are Grant Conroy and Ed Durston.

Second, Durston never mentions that he and Diane were standing together on the balcony when Diane suddenly became horrified because she believed the building's doorman was going to kill his dog. Instead, Durston tells Jameson that, out of the blue, Diane bolted onto the balcony and attempted to climb over the railing in an attempt to kill herself. These two accounting are substantially different because they serve different purposes.

Third, when Durston talked with Jameson, he made no mention whatsoever of the phone call made to Diane's brother Robert, as he told the investigators. The reason is because in the version Durston told Jameson, there was no long passage of time between Diane attempting to climb over the balcony railing and when she went out the kitchen window. In the version Durston told the investigators, this time lapse was established by Durston's claim that he and Diane went to her bedroom and calmly sat on her bed.

In my view, it appears that Durston needed to account for the possibility that Diane's neighbor (her bedroom wall is the only shared wall in her apartment) may have heard him and Diane in her bedroom—perhaps not "sitting calmly"—but, more importantly, he needed that time gap in order to account for when the telephone call was made to Diane's brother (more on this below).

At this point, I feel it's important to share with the reader what Bobby Jameson told me a year ago when we were communicating about the people and events that led up to Diane's death. When I asked Bobby Jameson about Ed Durston, he wrote back, "Ed pursued everything and everyone for his own advantage. He was a sleazy dude. Diane was emotionally vulnerable because of her recent breakup with Harvey. Ed played on weakness, whether temporary or ongoing. I threatened him more than once regarding my girlfriend Nancy Harwood. I watched him like a hawk. Ed was a hard read. I never knew what he was really thinking or doing . . . negative vibes . . . but in a way I never encountered in anyone else."

EIGHT

october 4, 1969 revisited, part 2

When I first heard the explanation of what occurred on the day Diane died, it made me uncomfortable. Knowing what I know today, I'm considerably more uncomfortable. The following scenario is surely not entirely correct. It is, however, a more logical interpretation of the available information. At the very least, it discredits the notion that Diane Linkletter had a serious drug problem dating back to her early teenage years and that on the morning of October 4, 1969 that she committed suicide because she was despondent, as it has been told for the past 47 years . . .

When the street party was wrapping up around 3 a.m., I believe that Ed Durston was at the party and offered to escort

Diane back to her apartment. Given the hour and that the area is a stone's throw from The Strip that is frequented by druggies, it's understandable that Diane would have accepted Durston's offer.

Upon arriving at Diane's apartment, Durston asked if he could come in for a while, and Diane allowed it. Once inside, the two talked, and Diane, being sociable, turned on the FM radio and offered to bake a tray of cookies. I don't believe at any time Diane entertained being romantic with Durston who, according to Bobby Jameson, was neither an attractive man nor Diane's type.

Although things went well for a couple of hours, my sense is that at some point Diane became tired and hinted that she and Ed Durston should call it a night. I believe this is where Durston's controlling, aggressive nature began to kick in. This is the place that Durston could get to that caused Bobby Jameson on several occasions to warn Durston to stay away from Nancy Harwood.

It had been only three weeks since Diane and Harvey Dareff broken up, and so in Durston's mind Diane is not only vulnerable, but available. When it becomes clear to Diane that Durston isn't leaving, his controlling nature begins to display subtle sexual overtones. Moreover, at this point, it's entirely probably that Durston made a sexual advance. Keep in mind that Durston was considerably bigger than Diane, who stood 5'2" and weighed 126 pounds.

To me, it makes more sense that this is when Diane called her brother and why she called him. I believe that she excused herself, most likely claiming she was going to the bathroom, and when she arrived in her bedroom, she, feeling anxious and perhaps even frightened, called Robert. This is confirmed by Dixie Dale, who was the telephone operator at the Shoreham Towers, who confirmed to police that Diane had called her brother and that Diane "sounded like she was on something."

In my opinion, Diane wasn't on drugs. She was scared. And the only reason that Durston told the investigators that Diane had taken LSD is because he needed to account for her hysteria. Surely, he couldn't tell the investigators the real reason she was out of control.

As an aside, if Diane truly were having a bad acid trip, which I feel is highly unlikely, all she would need to do was take a few of her codeine tablets that had been prescribed to her and were in her possession and go to sleep. And if she didn't know this, surely Ed Durston knew it. Being an opiate derivative, the codeine would have acted as a sedative.

The placement of this phone call in the timeline is critical. When Durston gave his accounting to Jameson, he failed to mention Diane calling her brother because this had occurred *before*—not after—he and Diane got into several physical confrontations.

When Durston talked to Jameson, he blamed Diane's attempt to kill herself solely to her being despondent, never mentioning her taking acid, being horrified by the doorman chasing his dog, or calling her brother and telling him that his sister took LSD.

In my view, the sequence of events that Durston told his friend Jameson were exactly as they happened. Hours later, after

Durston realized the flaws in the accounting he gave Jameson (who may have told others and surely could have been interviewed in the future by the sheriff's homicide investigators), he changed many of his statements made to the investigators to essentially explain several key discrepancies.

I believe it is reasonable to accept that Diane called her brother and told him that there was a man in her apartment who wouldn't leave and was acting aggressively toward her.

Upon hearing this, Robert told her that he would come over, essentially to remedy the situation. Unfortunately, offspring of high profile celebrities are schooled at an early age that, unless it's a matter of life and death, to never call the police or an ambulance when the situation could result in a media frenzy, but instead to call family. Had Diane called the police instead of her brother, there is a good chance she wouldn't have died.

It is at this point that I believe all hell broke loose when Durston suddenly realized that Diane had called her brother, who was now coming over. Durston flips out. This is a man with a police record, and if he had done something to Diane, he could go to jail.

As a footnote, according to Diane's autopsy, she had "a rather extensive laceration-contusion of her upper right lip." Considering that she landed on her head, primarily toward her forehead, it's unlikely that this would have caused what more closely resembles an injury from being punched in the mouth.

In addition, and perhaps of key importance, recall that when Durston was given a lie detector test, he was asked if he owned a gun. That's a curious question, isn't it? Is it possible that someone had told the investigators that Durston was in possession of a gun and that the investigators wondered if he may have had the gun in his possession on the morning Diane went out her kitchen window? Is it possible that in addition to running from Durston, Diane was running from a gun? Surely, this is pure conjecture on my part, but I couldn't help but wonder why investigators found it necessary to ask Durston that question.

At this point, Diane would be coming out of the bedroom into the living room. The front door is only entrance into her apartment, and Durston would have been standing between Diane and her only escape route. I believe at that point Diane feared for her safety and bolted onto the balcony because it was an open area where she could have been seen by others (mainly people in the apartments across the street) and could have been heard if she screamed.

Diane bolting onto her balcony and becoming hysterical is exactly what Durston told Jameson, only in my view, her hysteria had nothing to do with the building's doorman chasing his dog.

From this point, the events continued to unfold exactly the way Durston conveyed them to Jameson. He dragged Diane back into her apartment, most likely covering her mouth, and threw her onto the living room floor. Realizing the precarious situation she was in, she managed to convince him that she wasn't going to cause trouble (Durston spun this to claim she told him her climbing onto the railing was a joke) and he let her up.

It's at this point that Durston knows he has a serious problem. One, Diane's brother is on the way, and two, it has occurred to him that it's entirely possible that someone may have seen Durston fighting with Diane on the balcony and called the police. As a footnote, it's important to note that Diane's apartment was a corner apartment that had only one common wall—the east wall of her bedroom. Once that bedroom door was closed, she could have screamed at the top of her lungs and no one would have heard her.

Durston's mind is now spinning, and he needs to get Diane to agree to keep her mouth shut about what has transpired, which may have included assault and attempted rape.

Although it's impossible to know with certainty how Diane responded, it's fair to assume she may have felt more secure now that her brother was close to arriving. As angry as she must have been, it's possible she got in Durston's face.

Clearly, whatever transpired at this final stage between Durston and Diane didn't go well and, in my opinion, resulted in her again trying to escape from Durston. With him blocking her bedroom and the front door, she ran to the only place left—the kitchen. Upon making it there, she leapt up on the kitchen counter with the intention of screaming out the small kitchen window, thus repeating exactly what she minutes earlier attempted to do from her living room balcony.

In hot pursuit, Durston quickly catches up to Diane and attempts to drag her away from the open window, and in their struggle, she was propelled through the opening and fell six floors to her death.

Notice that I used the word "propelled" through the window. I did this purposely because this points to a major discrepancy in the version of events that Durston told Bobby Jameson. Remember that when Diane was falling through the open window that Durston told Bobby Jameson "I had a hold of her ankle, man, I had her by the ankle, but I couldn't hold her, I just couldn't hold her, man."

If it is true that for a while Durston had a solid hold on Diane's ankle, then this meant that her body, suspended outside the window, was literally lying vertically against the side of the building with her head facing down.

The problem with this is that Durston never told Investigator Hamilton that he had hold of Diane's ankle. Instead, he told Hamilton that he had grabbed for Diane's belt and, having missed, ended up holding a handful of drapes in his left hand.

Seemingly, the investigators had the same curiosity about Diane's last positioning just before she fell. The following is contained the investigator's report:

After the investigators finished working Diane's apartment, they "moved to the outside of the building and noted that at the west end there was a planter that measured approximately eight feet wide from the building to the sidewalk. Approximately two feet on the sidewalk was a pool of coagulated blood. This blood was approximately 30 feet north of the southwest corner of the building and an adjacent Edison Company light pole #1487245E.

"While at the location, the investigators performed an experiment using a cushion that weighed approximately 10 pounds and had a similar consistency to a human being. By sticking the cushion out through the window and then dropping it without using any force, the cushion landed approximately six inches from the base of the building. On a second attempt, the same cushion was propelled from the same window, using a certain amount of force. This time the cushion landed 12 feet from the base of the building at the same proximity of the previously mentioned coagulated blood."

What this simple test proves is that Ed Durston never had a firm hold on Diane's ankle while she was hanging out the window. If that were true, then at the time he could "no longer hold onto her," she would have fallen directly into the planter below, which didn't happen. Instead, she landed on the sidewalk, 12 feet from the edge of the building.

In my opinion, one of two things happened—either Durston grabbed Diane's ankle when she was standing on the counter, and when she immediately yanked it away from him, her momentum carried her out the window; or, alternatively, Durston, realizing he was potentially facing serious trouble with the police, pushed her out.

Personally, I'd like to believe the first alternative—that over the course of those final 15 minutes in Diane's apartment, things got so out of control that resulted in Durston's anger and frustration getting the better of him. Add to this, Durston suddenly being besieged with paranoia, and the result was that during a violent struggle, Diane accidentally fell through the open kitchen window.

While I would truly like to believe that Diane's fall was an accident, there is one nagging problem that occurred 16 years later that involved Ed Durston and actress Carol Wayne, the former blonde, busty TV personality and Johnny Carson's "Art Fern's Tea Time Movie Matinee Lady."

According to published reports, Carol Wayne was on vacation in Santiago Bay, Mexico with Ed Durston when the couple had an argument about where they were going to stay that evening. Durston checked into a hotel, and Wayne reportedly left to walk on the beach. That was the last time anyone saw her alive. A local fisherman found her limp body floating in the shallow bay waters three days later. Mexican authorities wondered how Carol Wayne came to drown in waters four feet deep, fully clothed. There were no cuts or abrasions, so a fall from the nearby rocks was ruled out. The coroner stated that death occurred days earlier and, as was the case with Diane, the body tested negative for drugs and alcohol. When locals went to look for Ed Durston, they discovered that he had checked out three days earlier, leaving Wayne's luggage at the airport with a message that she would pick up her bags in the morning.

In conclusion, it is my sincere hope that the time I have spent writing this small book will dispel the false rumor that during Diane's brief life, she had a serious drug problem and that she committed suicide because she was despondent over the direction her life had taken. Given all that I knew about Diane, coupled with all that I was able to uncover researching the last two years of her life, there is no question in my mind that on the morning she died, she had not taken LSD and that she was completely content with her life and looking forward to what surely was a bright future.

Diane was interred at Forest Lawn Memorial Park, Hollywood Hills, California, Enduring Faith section. Her tombstone reads: "Darling, we loved you so much."

about the author

Tom Bleecker began his writing career in 1969 as a screenwriter for Hollywood director Blake Edwards. After nearly two decades writing for screen and television, in 1987 Bleecker co-authored his first book with Linda Lee, *The Bruce Lee Story*, which served as the source material for MCA Universal's motion picture *Dragon*. In 1996, Bleecker wrote a second book on Lee, a highly controversial bestseller entitled *Unsettled Matters*. After penning nearly 50 biographies, in 2012 Bleecker wrote his first novel *Tea Money* that was followed by *Big Band Star Maker* (the life story of Big Band leader Horace Heidt), *The Jet: The Benny Urquidez Story*, *My Song*, which is the story of Polish immigrant Jolanta Soysal turned New York socialite, and *A Life at Risk*, the story of legendary Hollywood stuntman Rick Avery. Bleecker lives with his wife Lourdes in Southern California. The author can be contacted through his website www.tombleecker.com.

Proof

Made in the USA
Charleston, SC
30 June 2016